IONS

OF MANIFESTATION

Simple steps to create

your heart's desires

and soul's purpose

TEZA ZIALCITA

Editing and Layout by Sheryl Jackson

Coediting by James Leard and Alma Bella Maglaya

Book Illustration by Patricia Barretto Lacap

Book Cover Design by Lunaya Shekinah

Page Graphics by Carla Gladman

ISBN-13: 978-1512119473

Lovingly dedicated

to all sentient

beings of light

who co-created

this beautiful

Universe

♡

CONTENTS

Acknowledgement

I am forever grateful for the loving presence and support of my soul friend, Mr. Alan Hawthorn. The beautiful expression of your love for me, "your presence is in my spiritual neurons!" is deeply embedded in my being.

To my loving spiritual companion Kevin Diakiw, thank you so much for all that you do to make my life's journey filled with compassion, love and kindness. You are my monk lover.

To my ever beautiful soul friend/editor, Sheryl Jackson, my heart is filled with joy and love for all the times we spent together. Thank you so much for sharing your words of wisdom and for your collaboration; you helped to make one of my dreams come true. "IONS" is so dear to me and you made it happen. You are God's gift and blessing in my life.

Thank you so much to my beautiful and loving Book Coach Pia, you are God sent.

Thank you so much Alma Bella Maglaya for our beautiful soul friendship and wonderful editing of my work. You are my miracle worker.

My deepest appreciation goes to the most loving and supportive Dr. Brian Rukavina. Thank you for all the loving care, knowledge and wisdom you've shared with me.

My deep appreciation and grateful heart goes to James Leard, one of my editors, for dedicating his time, energy and love.

My warmest gratitude goes to Lunaya Shekinah for coming into my lifetime as my divine, creative artist.

To the sweet and gracious Patricia Barretto Lacap, thank you so much for sharing your beautiful sacred mandalas to "IONS". You are such an angel.

Thank you so much Carla Gladman, for your finesse and final touch to complete "IONS". Your love and support are deeply appreciated.

To my soul sisters Susan Lee, Joy Jose, Tana Clarkson, Joanne Remillard, Gigi Ricarse, Suzanne Gonzales, Patricia Schneider, Lisa Webster, Jeanette Bernal- Singh, Kelly DelBianco, Suzanne Maslowski, Sharon Westler, Suki Lee, Marita Ulrich, Kim Wuirch, and Jane Crompton, your sisterly love means a lot to me. I'm blessed to have you all in my life.

To all my ever dearest friends, you know who you are …too many to mention. Thank you for unconditionally loving me no matter what. And, my co-workers from New Vista Nursing Home, thank you for the 24 years that we've shared caring for our dearly beloved residents. To all my residents that share their love, laughter and vulnerable moments with me.

To all the souls who come to my Akashic Records soul healing group, thank you for sharing your life's experiences, vulnerabilities, and love with me.

I'm very grateful for all my beloved family members; six brothers and three sisters. Especially my parents Manuel Zialcita and Ramona Zialcita, who are my Sacred contracts, without them I would not be who I am today.

To all my beautiful and loving children; Jasmine my sweet angel, Matt Zialcita, Theo Hill, Tiffany Hill and Tristan Hill, you are all my miracles and treasures in this lifetime. Thank you so much for all the unconditional love and lessons that we shared on our souls' journeys.

Thank you Lords of the Akashic Records, Ascended Masters, Archangels and angels, Saints, Benevolent beings of Light, my spiritual team and guides, my Higher Self, loved ones from another dimensions. Thank you, thank you and thank you. My life is a living miracle because of your presence in my lifetime.

Foreword

You Are the Creator of Your Life!

Our human species needs to wake up from the illusion of our creation. We are at the peak moment of the evolution of our consciousness. We are all responsible for our transition towards ascension. We cannot stay here and remain blinded to all the challenges and difficulties our collective consciousness creates.

We are a part of the bigger picture. We all need to be accountable for our participation, consciously and unconsciously. This is the time to realize that everything we think, speak, emote and do affects our consciousness as a whole, as one organism of the human species.

There is no turning back. We are called to lighten up and assist each other in transcending victim consciousness into empowerment. How can we contribute to this evolution? By being conscious of our own existence, to become aware of all our thoughts, words, emotions and actions in our Akashic fields. When we know that everything we do affects our Book of Life, which is our Akashic (Soul) Records, we become responsible and accountable for our existence. Thus, we affect the collective consciousness of humanity. We are building new realities for future generations.

We are the way showers. We are light workers. We work so that our darkness can dissipate and be one with all creation. We are the co-creators of all that is. When we connect to the Source, become magnificent beings of light.

Fear turns into empowerment. Fear gives us the courage to face every obstacle that we encounter. The doors open for those who are called to be leaders of this awakening. We are here to serve as pillars of light. We are here to share our knowledge, wisdom, and gifts of healing to humanity. Without faith, we can't be in the space of trust. Surrender and merge your ego with your true self which is Spirit. Creation starts with the energy fields. Everything is energy. Our souls have reached this awakening to reveal to us how we can be conscious co-creators with the Universe.

The 'Ions of Manifestation' is an invaluable spiritual tool. We start with an intention to declare what we want to create in our life. By declaring this intention we sign an agreement with Source. Our faith will lead us to our creations. The next step is to clear our vision and make it free of distractions. We visualize that everything is already here. This is walking in faith. Walking in faith facilitates an allowing and a surrendering to the force of the Universe. Next, we focus our expression in creativity, with attention, with clarity. Where we put our attention, energy flows.

Then, last but not least, we take action. It is very important to be an active participant in our creation with the Universe. The universe will test us and give us situations that will push our buttons to show us how we truly want our creations to manifest.

Integrity is a big part of aligning our heart's desires and soul's purpose. Every aspect of our true self will be purified and the fire in our spirit will determine the outcome.

Trust in the Universe, everything is here! We are already in the Universal energy. Creation manifests when we are aware, awake, aligned, and activated to our truth. Our Universal conscious selves, spiritual guides in multi-dimensions, and beings of light and love, will lead the way for us toward an amazing life. We are here to manifest our authentic selves. We are here to be in oneness with all that is. We are here to live in peace, express joy and love, and be in gratitude for all the blessings that we receive. It is time to wake up, help others, share our gifts, brighten our light and experience the gifts of our Universe. There is no time to lose. We are being called to a bigger purpose, to become one with all that is. By creating love, peace and joy in our Akashic fields, we will accelerate the ascension process. We will then walk, in our lifetime, fully awake and conscious of our golden light, here to experience being human, and fully loving every moment.

When I first started writing this book, initially, it was only about sharing the steps that I took when I manifested my first book, Universal Conscious Self. But, now I've found that as I've been going through my soul's journey with the Akashic Records in order to write this book, meeting my phenomenal spiritual gurus along the way has been an amazing experience! It was such a blessing to spend five incredible days with Garchen Rinpoche, Sakya Trizin and the Dalai Lama to take refuge with their teachings.

It was so humbling and grounding, just to be in their sacred presence. I was enveloped with love, inner peace and joy in my heart. Their teachings were about mindfulness, compassion, kindness and no harm to all sentient beings. I believe we are all one in these Universal teachings when we connect to one Universal mind of creation. Everything is bonded by love when we attune to the awesomeness of our existence.

Whoever is your teacher or mentor in this lifetime, feel blessed to have them in your presence. I'm very blessed to have such eye opening teachers...with all my humility and gratefulness, I thank you for coming into my lifetime!

May this book inspire all sentient beings who have come in touch with my work.

May the Source of Divine light ignite the spark in your heart to shine and be a light to others on their journey. I pray that the Source of all creation be with you in all of your creations and that you be protected in every way.

Blessings of miracles,

Teza

INTRODUCTION

Manifestation of Our Higher Selves

There are many consequences which can occur when we are not happy with our lives. Those might include: toxic relationships, lost loved ones, financial instability, physical and mental illness, or other forms of suffering. What we need to understand is that at Source, we are beyond these situations and that we have the power to shift and look at them in a different light. As an Akashic Records Healer, I see clients coming from all different perspectives of their shadows and ego. We are here to manifest our Higher Selves, meaning whatever situations we are in, we have the power to align and connect to our highest potential. We can make the best of our current experiences.

It can be difficult to shift these perspectives because we are living inside our head (or our ego mind). That's why the practice of meditation can help clear the toxic thoughts created by our egoic mind. When we open and heal our wounded hearts we become an open portal to magnetize magnificent things, like love, peace, abundance, joy, and miracles! We start to attract beautiful situations and experiences that replace our current patterns of pain and suffering. To come into this space, we have to know, understand, and love ourselves.

The Universe will provide when we ask for help. The simplest way to access this is just by asking. "Ask, and you shall receive" — so very simple, yet so profound.

The steps to manifest our Higher Selves will be explored in the following chapters:

1. INTENTION: Intention is the foundation of our creation. We are the creator of our manifestations. Everything is here. All we need is here. Everything is energy, vibration, and consciousness. Everything is a mirror of who we are. We are the magnet of what we attract. The key is learning how to attract what we want and letting go of what we don't want.

We are always connected to the Divine energy and soul. When we shift the way we see our true selves, we will manifest the beauty and love of life in all ways. This is our birthright! By radiating our pure awareness and light, we will attract people that are on the same wave length. We will, in turn, become a light for others to see their Higher Selves.

By surrendering to the call of our soul, we find our path. We are on a journey that is unique to ourselves because we have co-created it with Source. Allowing life to flow as it is and surrendering to whatever is presented to us in the present moment will help us pave the way to enlightenment. We must clear our minds to reveal our inner selves. Ask for assistance from the Ascended Masters, Archangels, angels, and spiritual guides, to guide us in manifesting our highest potential.

2. VISION: Like a blueprint, we have the power to create a vision of our future in the present moment. Vision is the tool that will guide us in our creation. Remember that everything we need is within us. We are aligning with our Higher Selves within the quantum fields to manifest at a higher vibratory state. Our vision will come together like pictures glued to the pages of our Records in the Akashic fields. Every time we are connecting with our Higher Selves, we are rewriting our soul's Akashic Records. A clear vision is important to define what we really want; it is our heart's desire that will create strong, magnetized fields of attraction to what we want to manifest.

3. ATTENTION: When we want to manifest something, it is important to be focused and clear. We need to be in alignment with our intention and focus on what we want to manifest. Where we put our attention is where the energy flows. It becomes the channel for manifesting from our Higher Selves. Our discipline, focus, concentration, and dedication will determine the result of our ultimate goals. Attention on our Higher Selves will beam this light force toward the desired manifestation.

The following acronym can be used as a practical tool and guide for our manifestations:

FACE: F for Focus, A for Attention, C for Creativity, E for Expression (see Chapter 3 for more information).

4. ACTION: Action is an important factor for manifestation. Our soul's intention along with the Universal energy, infused with action, creates manifestation. The amount of conscious effort we contribute will determine the outcome. If we want to create something, we have to move with the flow of energy in a state of non-resistance, this is the key to manifestation. Our passion is the tool to ignite the fire within our hearts, fueled by our soul's purpose. We have these gifts right from the beginning, but our ego has concealed them. We are now being called back to the Source by reopening our hearts to what is now. Our consciousness is expanding into the understanding of our truth. Our heart is the vortex of everything, and when we stay open, we are loved. Self-love is the doorway to our Higher Selves and our purpose here on Earth. We are living multi-dimensionally by becoming consciously aware of our truth and existence. With this realization we become empowered to use our gifts and become beacons of love and light for those who are still asleep to their own truth. When we become aligned to our Higher Selves, we manifest our truth and can serve others in their soul's journey.

TEZA ZIALCITA

CHAPTER 1 | INTENTION

Universal Fields of Energy

We are tapping into the Universal fields of energy when we are putting our intention "out there". The Universe is in suspended animation. Our intention creates motion. Our intention attracts things to us that are in alignment with that intention. The gift of knowing this, is that you have the power to create whatever you want. We are multi-dimensional beings simultaneously travelling into many dimensions and parallel lives. When we want to create something in the future we have to know that it is already here; this is the quantum leap. Where our attention goes the energy flows.

Our physical reality is composed of subatomic particles that are in our subconscious mind. When we tap into our subconscious, we are aligning ourselves with our highest potential. We must not be distracted by any unconscious negative beliefs of our ego mind or other false realities; they are not aligned to our positive light and pure awareness. The Universal fields are full of limitless possibilities of our Higher Self. Knowing that we have this birthright, we can reclaim our power and be who we want to be. We don't need to be small; we are as big as the stars in the sky!

When we are aligned to the Universal fields of energy, we attune to the synchronicities of our reality.

We realize that everything external is reflecting that with which we are in alignment with.

By creating from our soul's blueprint and allowing the flow of God within us, we naturally tap into our multidimensional selves. By being aware of the people that we are attracting into our reality, we are given the opportunity to learn lessons from these relationships. When we are in this awareness, we are embodying our God essence.

Awareness is the tool to our ascension process and manifestations. For example, if we are feeling shame or guilt we are vibrating at a very low emotional frequency and our awareness is disturbed. Without moving beyond these emotions, we are caught in a cycle of suffering. However, as we become more conscious, we can heal our sufferings and raise our vibrations, empowering us to manifest with more ease and grace.

Our reality is coded within the blueprint at the subconscious level of our mind, which is often buried deep within. How we view the world will define the summation of our experiences and projections in our everyday lives. We create our own reality when we are awaked to this consciousness. We become aligned to all that is. We become present and aware of our spiritual lessons at this very moment.

When we think inside the box, we are contracting this Universal energy within our own perceptions of the world. We lose touch with our expansive selves. In order to expand, we need to contract just like anything else in this world.

The only way to expand our consciousness is to experience what contraction means. This is when we become like puppets to our own thought patterns and unconscious negative beliefs about our own existence. Embedded within the collective consciousness are countless beliefs of how our reality should look and feel. These beliefs are programmed into our minds through society; religion, media, political and economic systems, to name a few. All of these beliefs are rigid perceptions of what the world should be like. They influence our ways of thinking in big ways. We have to dig deep into our subconscious mind to see how we operate in our patterns of thinking and then shift our outdated belief system to one that cultivates love, peace, joy, and abundance.

To think outside the box, we need to have a quiet mind and be fully present in that space of peace. In order to achieve this, first we need to acknowledge our disorderly lives and chaotic minds. We cannot shift if we don't recognize that our mind is always chaotic because of the voices that continually come and go within our mind's consciousness.

Some thoughts can be like a ghost that haunt us in the middle of the night. We choose to be at peace with ourselves in order to find solace in this situation. The ego speaks so loud we can barely hear our truth and this crushes our spirit. Meditation is a tool to guide us to see the workings of our thoughts and release them.

We can develop the ability to observe our thoughts and not identify or react to what they are saying. Thoughts are usually there because of our previous experiences. In the past, we seem to have needed these voices to protect us from harm. However, now that we are becoming empowered at the soul level, these voices have served their purpose and it's time to let go of their false power. The only power that holds truth is love, not fear.

Our mind needs to be in a state of peace to bring order into our lives. A silent mind can bring about the shift from fear to peace. Fear is created within our mind by our thoughts, and it is our responsibility to shift these fear-based thinking patterns. Total transformation does not exist within the field of mind-consciousness; we need to shift to a different level or dimension. This is when meditation helps us to see the movement of our thoughts; the mind must be in absolute quietness to bring about the order that we desire. When we transform our fear-based thoughts, we become free. This freedom demands responsibility and requires order and discipline. We must learn not to conform to what society or others want us to be. We have the freedom to shift from a contracted state of being and align to our true expansive selves.

When our mind-consciousness expands outside the constrictions of our box, we can then tap into the vast Universal account of Source. We become a non-reactive observer to the drama and conflicts we were previously caught up in. We are limitless, with infinite possibilities of our highest potential. Expansiveness itself and live in the multi-dimensional Universe of our existence.

We are soul empowered beings operating within our hearts, burning in fire and passion to share this gift with others. We tap into the subconscious fields of our mind and co-create with our Divine soul's life, full of love and light. Cleared of the dramas and conflicts within ourselves and amongst others, we can establish a clear connection to the fields of the Akashic Records. We become cleared of our karmic cycle. Our level of vibration is accelerated to its highest frequency. We elevate into our higher consciousness, and bring this light to others, knowing that living from this space of love and light is possible. This experience of our true nature is the expansive energy that operates within our own souls when we are open and become the observer of our present moment.

If we are constantly faced with undesirable experiences in life, we must first recognize the patterns that are playing out. Then we can ask questions that will invoke changes in our fields of energy like *"what is the pattern that needs to be released?"* or *"am I ready to release these negative thought patterns?"* These types of questions will create awareness of our unconscious negative thought patterns which are creating the undesirable experiences.

Remember, we are the magnets of our own situations. There is no one else to blame. The other person in a situation is just a projection of our unconscious thoughts.

We need to ask ourselves if we are ready to face our fears and have the courage to feel the deepest truth underlying the core issues of the cyclical patterns of our lives. We need to learn how to stop and listen to our inner thoughts. We need to realize that whatever we see in others is what we have inside ourselves.

Everything is a reflection of who we are. The answers to the questions about our experiences with others lie deep within ourselves. We are unconsciously attracting certain people into our lives to learn more about ourselves. This understanding will bring light to our own shadows. This understanding will allow us to be at one with others in their own shadows. Only then we can deeply understand that we are all one in this field of consciousness; *they are you* and *you are them*. Meditate and look within your heart allowing compassion and wisdom to enter.

We put attention on love, commitment and intention to bring in harmonious relationships with ourselves and others. When we are empowered to experience that which is beyond our ego mind, we can tap into the force and power of the Universe throughout all aspects of our lives. Our emotional awareness and responsible choices regarding our authentic power will bring us into this space. Going with the flow of abundance and harmonious living, and becoming consciously aware of our powerful existence, we become in tune with the Universal Laws. Our contraction serves us in knowing our expansive selves in the Universal fields of life. It facilitates our becoming who we are supposed to be, in serving others, and in loving our existence in this multidimensional way of being.

Universal Mind

The Universal mind is a power house within us and all around us. When we tap into the power of the mechanism of this Universal mind, we will be in alignment with the force of God's love. Our brain is an instrument of the Universal mind. It is from this organ that we build, create, and think. When we are aware of how this mechanism works, then we can align with the power of the Universe to create and construct. We are tapping into our deepest passion and the fire which ignites our souls, in order to be what we are meant to be. It starts with putting our focused attention on what we want to create. Without this focus, our energy will be scattered and wasted. We need focus in order to harness our potential and bear the fruits of our intentions. With daily meditation, we can achieve our creation and become co-creators of this lifetime. Meditation, visualization, and feeling our emotions, are all effective tools in manifesting.

The Universe works in harmony and synchronicity, and the Law of Attraction assists us in manifesting something from nothing. We are co-creators in this vast Universe. We all have limitless potential to participate; this is our own true nature and our birthright. We are here to experience love, peace, and happiness. Our collective thoughts are what creates our external reality; it is only limited by our own creativity. Allowing the flow of this creativity will help yield fruits of wisdom. Our expansive selves know that we are connected to the Source.

We are always provided for and supported by this Universe that we inhabit. Our mind is capable of creating anything that we want as long as we are in the flow of the Universal energy.

Our brain is part of the nervous system that is comprised of neurons and transmitters that relay messages, informing it of our intentions and our current state of functioning. When we realize the importance and central role of these neuro-transmitters in communicating our intended realities, we can predict the outcome of our cause because the effect is what we have put into these data banks. Everything that is in harmonious relationship works in a functional mode, and this is how we should create and be in this lifetime. When we are in the natural flow of our system, we move in balance towards the results that we desire.

The subconscious mind is where the programs of our negative and limiting beliefs reside. These beliefs and thoughts can be quite deceiving. When we become aware that our reality is directly influenced by them, then we can correct and transform them into positive outcomes. The subconscious is the foundation of our life. We have to be aware of these thoughts to be in congruency with what we want to create. When we become aware, we wake up from our own illusions and we connect to our true selves. We came to this planet to experience our truth, which is love and happiness. When we achieve inner peace, there is nothing that can disturb us. This inner peace, achieved from detachment of false forms, or false ego, is true personal mastery. The result is alignment with our inner selves, which is spirit. This brings change to the way we view our lives and others. We become a vessel of light; one with all that is. The radiance of this light expands into the darkness and creates a luminosity that is quite transparent to the naked eye of those who see. You become a beacon of light and love in your field. You are at one with the Universe.

The Super Conscious mind is the source of your power and wisdom; here you connect to the Universal or Cosmic mind. The Solar Plexus is the seat of our wisdom. It is here that we generate light and the courage to bring that light into our energetic fields. Be aware of your gut feelings as they speak from the unconscious thoughts. These are the subliminal messages that we need to tune into to be free from the illusions of the ego. Our physical form is just a shell that acts on behalf of the spirit. When we are blocked, we are stuck in the egoic mind and we have difficulty living a peaceful life. When we are not harmonious within our own flow of consciousness, we become blind to our true essence. We unconsciously create situations that bring chaos, conflict, and pain. People continue to blame others and hold them responsible for their misery, but the truth is they draw to themselves such situations. They are asleep to the truth of their reality.

As observers of this drama, we will not emotionally react because we have shifted into our new selves, which are free of the radicals and toxins that hide our inner light. We become free to see the drama as it plays out in our external reality. We will be able to bring peace in the midst of chaos by just being there as a presence and a source of love and light. Compassion takes over our whole being as we become aware of the unnecessary human-mind conditioning that is not in alignment with the spirit. There is a sense of knowing that we are one, even in the midst of separation. Our senses are heightened to the energetic fields that are not in congruence with our souls and we become a beacon of light to help others find their path.

The Universal mind connects us to the Collective Consciousness of all that is. It is here that we connect to our Higher Selves and become aligned with our truth. There is oneness with others, and as we embody this inner peace and solace, we are moved to help others in their ascension process. Since the Universal mind is omnipresent, we are co-creating in the present moment, our future reality, in agreement with our soul's highest potential. Every spark of awareness brings light, hope, and faith to our new world in this era of enlightenment of the human species. We evolve as one mind collectively in many bodies as we exist in this third dimension. When we accelerate our frequencies to the higher vibrations of living multi-dimensionally, energetically speaking, we also increase the vibration of our planet Earth to match those of the Galactic Universe.

Everything that we see is a fractal part of the Universal self that we are. There is no separation between ourselves and others, as we are all one in this unified consciousness.

What is Our Souls Purpose?

The Universal energy is calling us to surrender to 'what is' and live our soul's purpose. What is our soul's purpose? Ask this question and surrender to what arises. That deep inner voice is there to guide the ones that are ready to listen. When we tune in, it's like our soul's fire igniting within, singing out to us that it's time to shine. It's time to let go of fear and fly.

Allow this fire to burn away the egoic thoughts that try so hard to identify with and cling to this illusion. We are born to shine our magnificent light, but first we must discover where we are blinded. Where are we stuck in our creativity, manifestation, and abundance? We are not here to experience lack. We are star beings experiencing humanity in this third dimension. The abundance that we inherit from this Universal and cosmic energy, or love, is within us. It is deeply encoded and rooted, just like a tree with strong roots. We need to be grounded to our Mother Earth "Gaia" to be able to grow strong, abundant, and empowered.

The hidden blockage that affects most human beings is their own ego. Our attachments to false illusions will only hinder our own soul's purpose. As blind as a bat, people walk without their fire ignited within; they are like zombies in the darkness.

The light that is calling them from within is constantly flickering, awaiting their transformation in order to connect them back to their truth and soul's purpose.

The veils have been lifted for all of us and the angels are here to support and provide us with our truth. Our souls are yearning to create more beauty, peace, and joy within. Our souls are yearning to radiate that beauty, peace, and joy to others whose lives we touch.

When we listen in silence, we can hear the calling to this space of love, to finally connect to what is, and what this life is all about. When we came here, we thought to ourselves, is this life? When we experience suffering, we ask ourselves, why do we need this? When we are rejected, sad, or abandoned we ask ourselves, why did they do these things to me? When we became the abuser, we ask ourselves, why do I do these things to them?

We are awakening to all of these actions and emotions. Now is the time to wake up and see that within each of us is the victim, the abuser, or the warrior. These are archetypes, or energetic imprints, within our psyche. We are not aware of these energetic imprints until we see within that we all have the same energy that' has been within us since the dawn of time. When we are awake and open to these energies, we become aware of our own inner self and which archetypal energies we are carrying. Then, we become wise to all our thoughts, words, and deeds. We consciously find these energies in our field and become aware of how they function and affect us. The awareness that we cultivate will become the guiding light on our journey.

This new consciousness of the Universal and cosmic energy becomes our space.

These teachings are revealed to those that are ready. In our search for love, joy, peace, and freedom, we will be provided with that which is relevant to our journey. The so-called "truth" is relative, meaning it varies for different people, dependent upon the illusions that are implanted inside their mind. So, whatever level of understanding we are at will affect our interpretation of the present moment and how we move forward. What is new today may be old tomorrow. There is no time and space in these new teachings of consciousness and the only barriers are our own selves. When we totally surrender to these teachings, we allow space, liberation of the mind, and freedom of the spirit. The soul's purpose is hidden within, and this is the treasure that we are searching for. This is why it is so important to move inward until we find what we are looking for.

Our destination is a feeling of wholeness. The healer that you are looking for is within you. You magnetized everything that is on your plate. Within you is the magnifying force that is the secret to all these teachings. When we stop searching, we find stillness and contentment within. When these two qualities arise, we create a magnetic field of force that will call all Masters to gather around this sacred circle that we created. This is where we unite with our higher purpose. This is the point of no return.

The magical times are here calling you. Your inner child remembers the love, joy, and peace that you hold dear.

The moment we connect to this delightful energy, we will find lightness and fluidity in all of our endeavors. Lighten up and think back to the days of childhood, when anything can happen.

This is the calling of the Universe to return to child-like wonder. When one surrenders, it allows space and transformation to manifest from within, which in turn, affects our external reality. When we listen to this calling without any expectations and attachments to the outcome, we surrender to Divine intervention. This is when the gateway opens and we return home.

When I first went to see my Akashic Records teacher I heard a voice say "you are returning home." What a revelation! When I surrender my will, then, "thy will be done".

With my experiences, I have been through a lot of suffering, chaos, and drama, but through all of this I became a stronger person. I never gave up on my dreams and passion, which is to help others transcend their suffering, chaos, and drama. Give hope to others, so that, even in the midst of chaos, there is that space that we can tap into, and feel that we are loved, and that everything progresses forward.

We are transient beings. Everything that is given to us is but a stepping stone to help us become stronger enlightened beings. By surrendering our power or control, we are allowing the path to unfold naturally.

Life's beauty and miracles start to knock on our door, opening a new dimension, not one of struggle, but of happiness and true peace.

It is difficult to give up control because we feel insecure when we are not in control of relationships, things, and places. Our egos are so noisily controlling our minds that we are not able to listen to the small voice, our pure spirit.

We are all one. The contracts that we made in the spirit realm bring all the wonderful souls onto our path. Can you imagine that we are all connected and have one spirit, one mind, and one body? Oneness is my spirituality because I believe there is no separation, nor duality, nor division in this life. If we listen and choose to surrender to that deep, passionate service, or calling to humanity, we are all working in unison for the ascension of our souls. When we connect to our soul's purpose we are in unison with the one Divine truth, we are one consciousness; many souls in one body, or many bodies in one soul. What we do creates a rippling effect within our soul's consciousness, and it is in this soul's bank, as I call it, that we put deposits. We make withdrawals, so to speak, when we create negative energetic imprints in our daily lives. What are we putting in this Universal bank? Have you looked at your life this way? Creating from within and connecting to all, we become conscious beings.

This is the wisdom that I found in my searching; what I see externally is within me and what I think about internally manifests externally.

What others experience is a part of me as well.

When I connect to this space of oneness, I find inner peace, belonging, allowance, unity, and harmony. This revelation has been with us for eons of time, but we are too blind to see because of our unconscious mind. Now that this wisdom is being revealed to us, we will find inner peace, joy, and unconditional love for all sentient beings. Everything that we touch becomes a part of this awakened consciousness.

Blueprint of Our Soul

When we incarnate here on Earth, we have the blueprint of our soul in the realm of the Akasha. These are the Akashic Records of our soul's evolution. From the time we leave the Source of love and light and incarnate to Mother Earth. The moment we are conceived, we are encoded with our soul's blueprint. Everything is energy, and when we open our Akashic Records we receive energetic downloads and healing. We are like an electric cable plugged into the source of electricity. Our electromagnetic fields are being re-calibrated into the light beings that we are. We are shifting and remembering our multi-dimensional existence. When we have access to our Akashic Records, we connect to our highest potential in this lifetime. Our energy centers are aligned and we live in multiple dimensions. These Records can only be accessible when one's heart is ready to heal and forgive. This is the link to our Divine selves.

We are here to remember where we came from. The Ascended Masters and angels are here to assist in the awakening of humanity. Those that are remembering, are now awakening to their truth. We are light beings and when we activate these light codes in our DNA, we learn how to fly again. We become fearless and empowered. We become aware of our soul's intention and why we are here.

The process depends on how a person chooses to let go of their ego. Detachment is a part of this process. When one loses their attachment to the materialistic world, they become aware of their consciousness. Then, their ego merges with the spirit and becomes one with the soul to fully embody their light codes, allowing them to live in their highest potential. There are limitless possibilities to what a person can do in this lifetime. The result of this evolution will bring inner peace, joy, and bliss. There are no judgments or fear, only love.

There are so many paths of attaining awakening and enlightenment. They are all directed towards inner peace, harmony, grace, love, and happiness. When we welcome and embrace everything in life, we become one in our "I am-ness". The sufferings of humanity will be lifted when we shine our light onto each other's paths. There is love in our hearts when we open and allow healing to take place. Let go of resistance and know that all is well. Whenever emotions trigger us, we can use the situation as an opportunity for transformation, opening the door to inner peace and healing.

Allow these transformations to release negative cellular memories and create a new you. Our existence will be shifting into the multi-dimensional beings that we are. We will live in parallel dimensions of ourselves. In this realm there is no time and space. Everything that we want to create is here right now.

We are bringing our future selves into this physical reality that we are grounded in. Remembering our soul's blueprint will give us guidance into living with no time.

We will magnetize all the magnificent experiences that we want to create. We are co-creating these experiences with all the Ascended Masters, light beings, spiritual guides, Archangels and angels that surround us. We will experience ascension in our physical bodies. We will become a conduit for energy to run through and help others to heal.

The messages will be given clearly, in Divine timing. We will be receiving guidance and direction for our expansion. We become a beacon of light from the Source of truth. This will help us see the blind spots or shadows that the ego is hiding from humanity. The healing comes through our hearts. When we open the portal of our heart, we allow our walls to go down. These walls prevent us from shining our true light. We can ask Archangel Michael and the blue flame to heal the area around our throat chakra so that we can speak our truth and make clear decisions in life. We can also ask that any cords of attachments be cut, and blockages from all timelines, dimensions and realities. We are aligning our heart and mind to create and manifest our Higher Selves. It is this bridge that will connect our ego to our soul.

We are light workers, here to shine our true light. When we shine, we help others in their shadows. We bring light into the darkness. It radiates love and grace. We become peacemakers and help others find inner peace. This is our soul's intention when we incarnate. We just forgot where we came from. We are in the awakening times, and accessing our Akashic Records will help us illuminate these shadows that are blocking us from embodying our Higher Selves.

Ask the Lords of the Akashic Records to open and guide us on our soul's path. We will receive downloads of information that sometimes don't make sense. There is no judgement, so release this fear.

Resistance is a sign of blockage. Reaction can trigger these emotions that are blocked energetically in our DNA. Surrender and allow the healing to take place. Our lives become much easier when we don't resist. There is a flow of abundance and grace. There is peace, love, and bliss. The more we access the Akashic Records, the more evolved we become. This healing will open the doors for our blueprint to manifest and create a beautiful life that is aligned with our true essence.

Trust

Opening our hearts with complete trust is quite a deep and wide door to open. To experience complete trust that everything will be alright brings us uncertainty. There is the feeling of "what if?" There is that skeptical voice that lingers around our head and tells us, do you really trust this person? When we are in a trusting intimate relationship with someone we become more open and vulnerable. Our weaknesses will then surface more easily, giving us a chance to recognize and deal with them.

Trust is such a treasure and so important to have within ourselves if we want to create pure and loving relationships with others.

As we shift away from our lower emotional vibrations, we become more aware of our feelings and our weaknesses. It can become quite confusing as we process our emotions. There are hidden triggers that will touch our core when we are in this space of confusion. Sometimes they are so subtle that we don't realize we are creating a wall of separation, a wall which blocks intimacy. Then, we have this wall that we are not aware of, until something triggers us to become defensive. We try to hide our truth and there's a part of us that wants to separate because that is the only way we know how to protect ourselves. The walls that we create to protect our vulnerable hearts becomes a tool for isolation, preventing true love in our lives.

In order to elevate these feelings of doubt and fear, we

have to open our hearts to realize that we are able to love and trust ourselves and others.

When our awareness becomes clear about what is transpiring, we can then connect and heal our emotional pain. We can feel the love and light that replaces our pain. The flow of this new love and light benefits our core being and our relationships with others. Trusting others is a leap of faith, that whatever happens in our experiences is what is meant to happen for us to learn and grow.

We cannot let the shadow of fear and doubt disillusion us from moving towards truth and love. The separation that we feel is our own creation which maintains our comfort zone in life. This comfort zone separates us from fear of the unknown. The lighted path of a spiritual warrior puts one face to face with their own shadow. Thus, we see ourselves with total kindness and compassion. Understand that we are here to learn, to master ourselves beyond the chaos and conflicts of our lives. Take every problem as an opportunity to delve into the abyss of the dark night of our soul.

We must listen to our hearts and completely trust in the unknown, surrendering our ego to be at one with the pain of our core being. When we face, embrace and accept our shadows, we integrate. We will see ourselves in a new light and feel true love. When this happens, trust for others begins to grow as we are able to trust ourselves to go beyond the fear and separation that we have created from others.

We are now embarking on a journey into a new dimension of our true loving selves. We are meant to trust our divine selves and others. We are love and light. Our perceptions of our new selves will bring alignment to our soul's true path. Shine this light onto others and feel love beyond measure. Together we will create peaceful, loving, and joyful lives.

CHAPTER 2 | VISION

Passion in Universal Life

"I am the expression of fire that ignites passion deep within my body, mind, heart, spirit and soul. I am now declaring to the Universe the expansion of my pure bright light, helping others on their soul's journeys." This affirmation helps with embodying expansion and manifestation in coordination with the Universal Laws. In manifestation, we need to be aware of our Sacred Contracts. These are vows, or agreements, that we made in past incarnated lives, as well as in the spiritual realm. The Sacred Contracts are energetically and genetically linked to our existence, although we may not be consciously aware of them. It is our cycle of repetitive patterns, dramas, and unresolved issues that blind us from our truth.

By being aware of our past lives and Sacred Contracts we are healing our cellular consciousness and DNA memory. We are becoming timeless, limitless, boundless, and expand into the circular motion of Universal and cosmic eternal time. There is no time and space. There are only fragments of memories built in our DNA bank of information. To heal incarnated past life vows, or contracts dwelling beneath our ego's mind control programs, we must surrender to these Divine Soul Contracts that we have. They are here now to manifest and experience, and surrendering to our Divine Soul Contracts is how we become a spiritual warrior of love and light.

To become a spiritual warrior, we have to be in tune with all our aspects of being, beyond our DNA, ancestral lineage and sacred vows. We become one with the Universal energy and light, as it penetrates our chakras, and we anchor this bright white light to the fields of our existence.

By creating our new wheel of sacred life, and integrating our body, mind, heart, soul and consciousness, we become open, ready to transform. Just like a butterfly ready to fly away from the cocoon of the caterpillar womb. We are but mirrors of these creations, which live in nature around us and remind us of our transformations and of the alchemy of the soul. Just like nature we are in a cyclical process of events. The soul is omnipresent, communicating with us at all times. We just need to be open to receive these Universal messages of sound, light, signs, keys, and coordinates in other words, codes of our blueprint.

When we become open, we allow ourselves to expand beyond our comprehension, becoming one with our cosmic or Universal soul. We start to soar like eagles in glorious flight, happy and content to be on top of the world. Learning our spiritual lessons and about our contracts will help us clear our energetic fields. When we receive insight into our karmic bondage, it opens us to the tremendous power of love and forgiveness.

We are then able to shift into being one with the Universal Laws. Everything begins to make more sense as we become one with God.

Anchoring our light into the heart of Mother Earth, Gaia, creates the expansion of our magnetic fields and allows the illumination of our truth to shine. We are in these holographic fields of matrices, now ascending, while remaining in our physical domains to continue regeneration at a cellular level within our DNA. This Ascension process will open doors of opportunities so that we may better understand the blueprints of our souls. Our compassionate love and wisdom will keep the Divine love anchored here to magnify our existence and connect us all to this life on our Mother Earth.

This fire that lights and ignites our true passion to live our purpose, will continue as we serve humanity in order for us to ascend into this magnificent light. Our magnified and illuminated souls will hold the high frequency and vibratory fields of Mother Earth as it glorifies and aligns to the Galactic center of our planetary ascension. The planet will continue to clear anything that does not resonate with this frequency as well as awaken others to their core cellular level of knowing.

This Universal light that holds the key codes in our cellular being will be activated and will hold this space of love. Ask **Archangel Metatron** to activate the Merkabah in our energy fields. The **Merkabah** (vehicle of light) will keep us protected along our soul's journey. It initiates us into the loving support of this Cosmic light and will guide those who are called to embody these light codes. Our cellular vibration will continue to rise up and allow these new key codes of light to activate. This is the time to illuminate and shine our most true bright light. There is no need to hide anymore. The chamber of light will keep us clear and radiating in our holographic fields of existence. We must shine this fire within our energetic fields and share the love of our soul's true desires in this lifetime. It's time to rise up and shine, exploring our limitless potential, and welcoming our bright star seeded selves.

It is important to surround ourselves with nature to rejuvenate our energetic fields and ground our soul into the heart of Mother Earth Gaia. When we are in touch with nature, it grounds us and balances our energetic fields. We are so bombarded with technology and noise pollution that we can't feel and listen to what is our truth anymore.

Call on **Archangel Sandalphon** to ground and balance our energy fields. We have addictions that hinder our awakening. Align our mind and heart to release addictions. Embracing our shadows creates self-acceptance to oneself and enable us to be empowered

Here and Now

In this Universal energy, we are all connected. There is no linear time and space. There are no boundaries or separation when we are connected to the Source of creation. We are truly magnificent beings of Light and Love. Everything that we experience in our reality is created within. Our awareness will bring us into this space of knowing. Let us open our hearts to heal and align with our magnificent selves, our pure essence of Light. Then we will become clear about our direction and what we want to manifest.

Call **Archangel Chamuel** and the Pink Ray of Light into our heart chakra to release, clear and heal our blockages.

In manifestation, we have to realize that we are bringing the energy of our future selves into the present moment. By being our authentic selves we experience our truth. Our presence is an oasis for others. We become a channel of love. Others are here to remind us of how beautiful we are. We are mirrors of each other. When we see others as mirrors then we are reminded of our fragmented parts. These aspects of ourselves bring us in touch with our multi-dimensional selves and we become aligned with our expansion.

Our expression of our true selves is our soul's purpose. We are here to experience joy, love, and peace. The here and now is where we are creating our future selves. We tap into our infinite selves when we know and understand our blueprint of creation. Then we can put our attention on our vision and know that it is here now. Faith is the quantum leap of our soul. When we have faith in our lives, it paves the way for things to run more smoothly. Trusting in the Divine order of things will synchronize events in order to create miracles in our lives.

When we present our intention to the Universe, it magnetizes things that are a vibrational match to us. Our vibrations will create our realities. We have to take responsibility for our own vibrations. Everything is our creation, whatever it may be. Everything we experience is here because we created it, consciously or unconsciously. Our awareness of where our experiences are coming from will help us transcend emotions that are of lower frequency. This is why it is so important to pay attention to what the Universe sends our way. Messages or guidance often comes in subtle signs and metaphors. When we are attuned, we will know because there is a flow. Have no resistance or fear. Don't judge whatever comes as there is always a bigger picture to see.

Let go of fear about anything, just be. Learn what the gift of our experiences is. We are the transmitters of communication of every kind. All sentient beings are capable of receiving communications. When we allow our hearts to open, it will become a portal to receive messages. All living beings and non-living things have access to communicate when we are open to receive.

Our limitations are created by fear. There are endless possibilities that humanity is capable of receiving. The secret door to this power is in the heart. This is how we access the Akashic Records and all the hidden doors of possibilities. The past, present, and future are in one unified collective consciousness in the realm of the Akasha. These doors, when asked to be opened, can provide us with information about our intentions. Allowing and surrendering to the gifts of the Akashic fields will elevate our human consciousness into the Divine. This is the Higher Consciousness or Higher Self. Tapping into the Akashic fields in the here and now will create our highest potential in this lifetime. The attachment to this reality will dissipate because we know this is just one facet of our creation.

The lesson is to not attach ourselves to lower vibrations, this will bring fruitlessness. Call upon **Archangel Michael** and the Blue Ray for protection and to cut the cords of attachments to people, places and things that are not serving our highest good. Flow with the emotions that arise and ask, "where is this coming from?"

Ask more questions. Let it soak in. Then we can shift these emotions which will transform us to become a more consciously aware person and find the bliss beyond the pain. Questions that you might consider asking are; what is the lesson? What is the gift? What is the role? What is the purpose? Am I ready to let go of this control? Am I feeling better? These questions can help transcend any situations that are not helping us in our ascension and manifestation. The lesson is to align ourselves to our highest potential, to feel good, and to become more consciously aware.

The here and now is the foundation of manifestation; being present and truly listening to what is happening in our energetic fields. What is being communicated? Every moment of our lifetime is a gift of knowing and understanding ourselves. Don't take these gifts for granted because they are here to awaken humanity. We are here to evolve into one unified consciousness where there is peace, love and joy. Every one of us is connected to everything that is happening in our realities. When we open our minds and hearts we can shift our consciousness into our highest potential. We are the ones who are going to create a world that is evolved and enlightened. We are ONE, and together we can be empowered to manifest wonderful miracles in the here and now. Believe in the power of love! Choose only love.

Opening to What Is

When we open ourselves to what is, we surrender our lives to limitless possibilities. We are the co-creators of our lives with the collaboration of the Universe. All you have to do is flow and surrender to what is. What is the expansive and infinitesimal dimension of our Universal self? We are unconscious to this vastness because we are asleep to our true essence. The awakening of the seeds of humanity is here. Everyone is here to experience this when we choose to do so. As a child, have you ever wondered about all of the wonders of the Universe? This curiosity, in itself, is the connection to opening the doors to our multi-dimensional selves. We go back to our sense of purity and innocence. We become alive again, full of vitality and energy. We become inspired to make a difference in the world and the lives of others. We are inspired to do beneficial things. This is the power of the Universal energy. We are in the unified consciousness of humanity.

Our intentions will make our visions come true when we take this first step. Visualize that your Highest Self is already here in the moment. Invite your creative energetic fields in to what you want to create. Surrender to the flow of the Universe and whatever is given to you. When you catch yourself in an energetic pull towards a situation or relationship, ask yourself, what is the gift in being here? You have created this in your field and it is meant to wake you up. When you see within, the lesson that you need to learn, you need only let go and choose love. The space of love will clear all that is not of use to your higher vibration. Allow only positive thoughts and align to your Higher Self. Your relationship with others is your barometer to your self-knowledge and wisdom. When you are able to see with these eyes of love, love follows you. The only lesson here is love. We just complicate things. Life is simple when we allow ourselves to be happy. Create from this wisdom of happiness and love. Things will fall into their right place. Don't concern yourself with others' problems; instead, focus on what you can do to be in the space of patience, non-judgement, and understanding.

When creating, we are in harmony with the flow and synchronicity of the Universal energy. To be in this space, we have to be congruent with our soul, which is Divine love for oneself. When we recognize this divinity or essence within us, we become awake to our existence. We become more aware that everything here in our life is a gift. We become more grateful to all that is. We create a space of unity, harmonious creation, and peace. The flow of love and grace in our lifetime will be felt within and we will come into a place of bliss. Opening to what is brings us inner peace that transcends our understanding of our existence. It gives us faith and hope to be in this blissful space of love.

Our purpose here is to love and live happily. This is what we signed up for, but we got lost in our ego and created suffering and separation. We go through a detachment process, which is knowing that we are souls experiencing being human. We become aware, and become the observer of our drama. After this separation, we become one in unified consciousness. We know that we are all fragmented parts of all that is. We are holographic beings living multi-dimensionally. We are connected to all that is. In the manifestation of our heart's desires and soul's purpose, we allow the flow of the Universal energy to shift us into our blueprint.

Opening to what is and surrendering to the flow of the Source involves becoming the observer of our creations, connecting to our blueprint, reflecting within, and releasing lower vibrations. By putting our attention on our essence and what we want to create, the Universal energy and Divine love will flow within and create a sacred space in our lives. We are able to manifest infinite possibilities and tap into our highest potentials in this lifetime. We are born magnificent beings of love and light!

The Power of Emotions

Our hearts are the power house for creation, combined with our alignment with the Universal mind of God. When our hearts are closed or blocked we are unable to tap into our vast and expansive nature thus creating a gap for our desires to come true.

What are these blockages around our heart chakra energy center? They come from energetic imprints and our Akashic Records. Unhealed or unresolved relationships with others, past lives incarnations, DNA, and ancient family lineage that we have inherited. These energetic imprints are produced from lower emotional vibrations such as anger, shame, guilt, and other unconscious conditioning or patterns of negative energy.

Our hearts hold the wisdom of our souls. When we open our hearts and allow forgiveness for others, we create the magical bond of love and oneness in our existence. Without forgiveness we are lost in the dark because we attach ourselves to the shadows of our souls. Our souls are light and they carry vast information which we can tap into. This information, or knowledge, translates into wisdom and finds a home within our hearts.

When we meet others for the first time, sometimes our heart beats fast like we already know these people. It is because our heart has consciousness and memories of our past lives, incarnations, and Sacred Contracts. We are meant to meet these souls in this timeline, or lifetime, because we made a contract with them.

Even if negative situations arise from these relationships, it is still a contract. Seemingly negative situations can become our greatest gifts if we learn from them and transcend ourselves as human beings. This is about finding the treasures in the darkness. We can find light in the darkness, which makes us beacons of light for others.

When we want to create, we have to start by identifying, which feelings do we want to feel? What makes us feel alive and vibrant? These feelings are our compass toward our soul's purpose and heart driven lives. When we connect and know these core feelings, our intentions for our creations become clear and free from distractions. We are being guided by our hearts and we are in the flow of the Universal energy. We become co-creators of our desires and we collaborate with the Source of creation.

Opening the Akashic Records helps us to release blockages and energetic imprints from our heart's consciousness. The vibrations of the Akashic fields will help us to evolve in our soul's growth and ascension process. It aligns us to our highest potential and highest good of all humanity. As we heal our heart and soul records, we create a rippling effect in our collective consciousness because our hearts receive this in our electromagnetic fields. It allows others who are vibrating at a lower emotional frequency to receive these codes of light and they become attuned to their own positive vibration.

Steps in opening your heart and the Akashic Records:

1. Create a sacred space for meditation, light a candle.

2. Call the Ascended Masters (whoever are your Masters of Light; it can be Lord Jesus, Medicine Buddha and many others), Lord Melchizedek, the Great White Brotherhood of Light, the Chohans of the Seven Rays, Benevolent beings of light, St. Germain and the Violet Flame, Archangel Metatron, Archangel Michael, Archangels and angels, spiritual teams and guides, loved ones from another dimensions, your Higher Self and body deva spirit to create a safe and sacred space for your highest good and healing.

3. Open your Akashic Records by repeating the prayer below.

4. "**Lords of the Akashic Records**, please open the book of (your full legal name) and create a safe sacred space. "I forgive myself consciously and unconsciously for hurting others. I forgive others consciously and unconsciously for hurting me."

Place your right hand on your heart and feel into it. Envision all the people that have hurt you in this lifetime and those that you have hurt. Send them love, light and forgiveness. We are also forgiving all our energetic imprints in all timelines, dimensions, space and realities.

5. Call upon **St. Germain and envision the Violet Flame** all around you and say the release prayer "I release any attachments, karmic bondage, beings, entities, souls, drains, hooks, cords, curses, unconscious negative beliefs, patterns, conditioning, bonding and blockages from all timelines, dimensions, and realities and ask that they go back to the Source of love and light. Let it be done with love and grace."

6. Scan your body, mind, heart, spirit, soul and other beings, be direct and simple tuning into your system. (i.e. Body – relaxed, mind – clear, heart – happy, spirit – inspired, soul – open, other being – angels around me).

7. Ask questions regarding your patterns or blockages from your Akashic Records. Journal and receive the answers.

8. Don't resist, judge, or fear what is given.

9. These messages are for you to feel and listen to. Allow this energy to flow in your body, mind, heart, soul, and spirit.

10. This is a very important part to close your Records after consultation. In order not to walk with your Records open, you will feel light headed and perhaps sick if left open. Thank the Ascended Masters, Archangels, angels, spiritual teams, guides, and your Higher Self for helping you. Thank the Lords of the Akashic Records for the healing and information and close the Records by saying; "The Records are now closed, the Records are now closed, the Records are now closed. Be it done with effortless, love and grace."

PLEASE NOTE: *This sacred prayer can only be used with those who are 18 years and older.*

The soul of a child is continuously growing and we do not want to disrupt their evolution and lessons in life. Thank you!

Surrender to the Flow of Universal Energy

When we surrender to the flow of the Universal energy, it sets the stage for the fruits of our intentions to manifest, whereas, if we resist, we are sabotaging our own desires. Like water, let thoughts flow, and know that the Universe will bring to us those who vibrate at the same frequency that we do. Everything that our heart desires is a magnet for attraction because the heart is the vortex or magnifier of all things; be it a relationship, money, or places that we want to travel. When we place our intentions, we are sending a signal to the Universal energy. Ions of molecular atoms will synchronize and harmonize themselves like glue to manifest our desires. Light attracts light, and our vision of who we truly are comes naturally to us as we become authentic with everything we do. Transparency is the rule of thumb; being honest with ourselves will help us to uphold our truth.

When we have faith in our vision, the Source will provide. We are a channel, or vessel, of this Divine energy. We co-create with this power of love. Love is the bond for things to manifest. For some, the biggest challenge is learning to recognize love, and accept every aspect of ourselves unconditionally. Then, we are embodying the light and living by example so that others can recognize the light within themselves. This is how we reach our full potential, in service for others.

When we surrender, we let go of attachments to the outcome. In this space we can enjoy the process and we will not be stressed about how things will unfold. It is a quantum leap of faith. The challenges that will come into our energy fields are our teachers for expansion and transcendence. Only, when we slow down enough, for our intuition and inner guidance to come forth, can we recognize and learn from these challenges. The key is to be more patient with ourselves so that we can be fully in the present moment. It is from this place that we learn and allow miracles to manifest.

Sometimes the path is not so easy to traverse when we are being called to our awakening. We will find ourselves in situations that are challenging. We will have to clear our energy fields. This first phase is one of purification. Some of these situations may include letting go of toxic relationships, grieving for our loved ones, and losing our material world. These trials will help us transcend our limitations and allow wisdom to arise. Our wisdom and connection to God is constantly communicating to us the ways to inspire our soul's purpose. We are being guided to listen to the signs that are given to us, leading us to doors that are opening for our expansion. We have to listen with an open heart and visualize the life we desire as if we already have it. Then we can surrender to the flow of the Universal energy with trust and faith, free of any doubt.

When we surrender we become happy, content, and humble to the gifts of the Universe. This serenity and contentment are treasures. We feel supported, loved by God and others. We become one with all that is. This is the blissful space of one's freedom of spirit. We are not consumed with what is happening with the world's affairs but, instead, our focus is on making a difference by sharing our truth, light, and love. It's about surrendering to the things that we can't change, and empowering ourselves to do the things we can to serve others.

CHAPTER 3 | ATTENTION

FACE: Focus, Attention, Creativity, and Expression

FACE is the acronym for focus, attention, creativity, and expression. When we want to manifest our heart's desires we have to pay attention to these aspects of creation. Focus is needed to propel the flow of energy to manifest our desires. When we are focused on a project, we have to practice discipline or routine to maintain the momentum of our project. If we look towards completing something in the future we must be practical about how we will subdivide our big project into smaller steps to avoid becoming overwhelmed.

Doing this also allows us to remain relaxed, happy, and focused. As we go through the process of creation, we will gain experience, as well as see the pitfalls of stagnation and procrastination. We will become more aware of what we need to do in order to stay focused. Prioritizing and making appointments is very helpful. This way we can set aside time for our own projects. Also, we must listen to our hearts and not the opinion of others if we want to maintain the focus required to achieve our dreams.

Attention becomes laser focused when we are able to be fully in the present moment of what we are doing. When we are in the flow, everything is in synchronicity with what we want to manifest. Where there is resistance, then there is a blockage to the energy flow. This is the time to listen to the body, mind, heart, spirit, and soul. Pay close attention to feelings that arise instead of running away from them. The deeper meaning to these feelings will be given through intuition, dreams, and gut feelings. Awareness is a big must when we are creating. Pay attention to the signs and symbols that arise in our daily life. The sudden appearance of people in our lives may play a key role in our transformation. Look for the deeper meaning of why these people arise in our lives. What can we learn? Knowing that everyone is a reflection of ourselves and that there is a reason we attract them into our lives, we can work with our external experiences to generate positive internal transformation.

Creativity is the hub of our passion. This is where the fire burns and makes our dreams come true. When we connect to our creativity we are with the source of life and creation. This is the zone of oneness. In this space we are aligned with the source. We can utilize this energy and the enthusiasm within to bring forth or give birth to whatever we want to create. Integrating our left brain and right brain, and activating our Pineal gland will connect us to our highest potential. The alignment of masculine and feminine energy will allow for our desires to manifest in a more balanced and harmonious way.

Expression is the outcome of our creativity at work. Expression at its fullest potential (expressing our highest potential for the good of all) is what results from connecting to our Higher Self's blueprint. In our blueprint we are connected to the source of creation. When we incarnate here on Earth, we have a connection to the Source, but most of us forget where we came from. As we align to our Higher Selves through the Akashic Records, we are also being activated to bring in the codes for our manifestation in this lifetime. The blueprint is like our memory of what we are to accomplish in this lifetime. It is our heart's desire of expression and creation. It is very important to align to our soul's purpose to live a fulfilled life. This alignment and awareness will bring the fruits of joy, love, peace, abundance, and miracles in this incarnation.

Where Attention Goes, Energy Flows

Once we become clear with our vision then we can directly focus our attention, which allows the energy to flow to what we want to create. It takes discipline and awareness to be in this flow. To manifest effectively we have to be in this flow of energy, moving toward our goals and creations without procrastination. It is passion that ignites the fire within and reveals our deepest desires in life. Be in this motion totally, ignoring what others think of you. We are here to manifest our desires with the cooperation of the Universal energy.

It is our attention which attracts things that will work with our desires, which is why it is so important to stay focused and free of distractions. Suddenly, we will meet people that will collaborate, support, and uplift us on our path. The Universe is a vast field of energy and we are a part of the Universe. It responds to the energy we put out. The summation of all our creations is comprised of all our heart's desires.

There is no limit to what we are capable of creating when we are attuned to the high frequency of the Universal energy. The Universal Law of Attraction can be understood when we learn to calm our constant thoughts to see through the illusion of our ego. Our positive thoughts create positive results and unconscious negative thoughts create resistant experiences. When we feel resistance to our feelings and situations, this is a door to explore. Any challenge indicates an opportunity for expansion, since it is a movement of contraction within our fields of consciousness. Unknowingly, we are holding a lower vibration within our energetic fields which is the cause of the constriction. When we release this, it allows for expansion.

The energetic fields create what we have in our reality right now. Internally and externally, this is us. When we feel triggered by something externally, we must look within for the answers. When we turn our attention to what is not expansive, we can look at this situation as an opportunity to learn. We become an alchemist, transforming the conflicts within ourselves into wisdom and compassion. By doing this, we are shifting our attention to positive outcomes and building expansive ways of thinking things through.

Our attention, combined with action and collaboration, creates the blueprint of our manifestation within the Universal fields of energy. We are within the Universe and the Universe is within us. When we realize this in the core of our being, we become vastly expansive beings of love and light. We can then radiate this essence to help others remember their true selves. This positive flow of energy will transcend any blockage that is perceived as negative to our senses. Allow the flow of life, be aware, and believe that everything is already here, whether we can see it or not.

How do we know when we are out of alignment with the Universal energy? When we experience resistance or blockages to achieve our desires it is a sign that we are not aligned with our higher vibrations of love. By checking in with ourselves at this point, we can develop awareness of our resistant thoughts and emotions. We can then transform them into loving thoughts and emotions. Also, when we surround ourselves with positive and supportive people it is like adding more logs onto the fire of transformation. This helps in the process of letting go of emotions that are limiting or obscuring our joyful self from being ever present. As we develop awareness of that which does not serve us, we become empowered to free ourselves from attachments of any entanglements with others' shadows.

People come into our lives as reflections of our own shadows to teach us lessons. When we become aware of the lessons that are to be learned, the cords of attachment can be cut.

We are in the ebbs and flows of life, so we can't always control what we will experience, but we always have the ability to consciously make choices that are most beneficial for us and others. If we get caught up in the drama unfolding around us, we can easily get lost in the illusion. However, through meditation, we can develop the conscious awareness necessary to be an observer of the drama without getting involved emotionally.

To manifest our heart's desires, we have to know what we want and be focused. This is why removing ourselves from the unending dramas of life is so important. It's amazing how fast we can lose focus, attention, and direction, when we engage in the dramas around us. When we state our clear intentions or desires to the Universe and flow with the current of life, free from distractions, manifesting becomes effortless. We are the writers, directors, and actors of this movie we call life, where our attention goes, the Universal energy of manifestation flows.

Think for a second: What makes me feel happy? What do I love to do? Where do I shine my light? These are some direct and grounding questions that can help in finding passion and in directing ones attention. By asking questions, we create a space for the Akashic Records to help us receive information that will be valuable to our self-inquiry. The information received are vibratory imprints of energy and our soul's Book of Life. This is how we tap into our highest potential and align to our souls' purpose.

Accessing our Akashic Records helps us to be in the flow of the Universal energy because we are tapping into our soul's Universal data stream. The records will reveal our blueprints, archetypal energies, past lives, and patterns that we want to address in this lifetime. When we are aware of our own records, we become conscious of all our thoughts, emotions, words, and actions. This has a great impact on understanding and evolving as a conscious soul within this physical body.

It's important that we become aware of our thoughts, vibrations, and attention as this will create the flow of our manifestations. When we allow the positive flow of light to vibrate in our energy fields, we attract positive and expansive experiences.

We can ask the Lords of the Akashic Records to open our Book of Life and reveal to us information that will help us transpire what we want in this lifetime. When we align to our own soul's records, we will evolve and be in tune with our highest potential.

Blockages to Manifestations

Why do we get stuck, not living our dreams? What is it that blocks us from manifesting what we want to create in this lifetime? When we are blocked we may feel like a zombie going through life without joy in our hearts. We will explore that which may hinder us in manifesting and connecting with our highest potential.

Most of us are unconscious or asleep when we are going through the motions of life without really putting attention on ourselves and what we truly want to do in this lifetime. We get caught up in the daily struggles of life believing that there is no other option. We forget that we are here to experience beautiful expressions of ourselves. These expressions will flow through us when we are aligned to the Source of everything. Being aware of our blockages is the first step to elevating and shifting our consciousness. It is in this field of awareness that we create the fertile grounds for positive transformation.

1. Procrastination:

Time is an illusion, we are living in eternal time and space. The Universe is in animated suspension. When we put an intention out to the Universe, it collapses and collaborates with our intention. But with this said, the most important aspect of creation is action. When we procrastinate we prolong the result of our project and create a gap between us and our desires. Every step that we take towards our desires attracts limitless potential and synergy. People who are procrastinating have a lot of excuses about themselves. They are in denial of something and they know deep inside that they are not ready for change. The antidote to procrastination is action. Do tasks daily that will contribute to the whole picture. When we divide our projects into smaller steps, we don't get overwhelmed.

2. Fears:

There is a lot of pain that a person can go through when they are paralyzed with fear. Fear of not being good enough can block a person from their creations because this unconscious negative belief is so deeply rooted within. Most of our fears have been passed down from family, society's demands and expectations of ourselves. These fears create insecurities that prevent us from fully embracing our gifts. They create dysfunction not only within ourselves, but also within family and societal structures.

Most of us are not born validated with our gifts and so we grow up seeking attention in the wrong places. We seek validation that we matter and that we are not limited. Some of us also fear success. However, we are here to experience success and fulfillment in all aspects of our life. Another aspect we fear is making mistakes; this can paralyze us from moving forward or taking risks. There is nothing to lose because we learn from our mistakes. Mistakes are the stepping stones to our success. We will make mistakes, but what if we see our mistakes as our guides towards knowledge and wisdom?

Some of us fear what others will think of us. We should not care what others think. We are unique light beings that incarnated to shine our light here on Mother Earth. The stem of this fear is insecurity and when we become aware of this, we can shift this feeling by loving ourselves more and by not being so hard on ourselves.

3. Lack of focus and clarity:

When we are not focused and clear about what we want, we are all over the place. Clarity gives flow to what course of action we are going to take. The path you're taking requires focus so energy can flow in that direction. This gives the Universal energy the power to work with our creations. It collaborates and sends us people or things that will help or support us with our heart's desires. We live in a supportive and nurturing Universe. When we know this deep in our core, we can then empower ourselves and others. When we work with this strong force within and around us, we become magnificent and radiant beings of light.

4. Priority setting:

We have to know our priorities to become aligned to our heart's desires. If we don't make a list of our priorities then we are lost in the vastness of the Universe. How can the expansiveness of the Universe produce what we want if we don't know what matters most in our lives?

Our priorities will eliminate the clutter in our mind. It will shows us what we should put our attention on and where to go from there. It is also important that we create from the heart. When we do this, we become happy and fulfilled. Our creations reflect what our soul's purpose is. When we know what our soul's purpose is, then we can prioritize the steps and tasks required to manifest our heart's desires.

5. Lack of faith:

Having lack of faith is a large blockage in manifestation. Without faith there would be no quantum leap. It is important to have non-wavering faith and believe that what we desire is already here. Imagine that we live on a blank sheet of paper where we can draw anything that we wish for. When we have faith in these creations, we will definitely have these manifested in our reality. But without faith we are not aligned to the Universal energy of flow because our energetic components are in resistance with what we desire. We are creating a vibrational mismatch with what we want to create. Things that we want have to vibrate in the same frequency as our energy. Everything is energy and consciousness; our thoughts, words, and actions, they all have to match our desires.

Shifting Blockages

In the process of manifestation we will encounter blockages or things that seem to hinder us from reaching our goals or destination. These are the experiences that will come into our awareness; they are the barometers on our way to success. We should pay attention to what these experiences are and transform them into creative solutions. Blockages are seemingly problems or illusions that will serve as doors for opportunity. Blockages are signs of misaligned energy. When energy is not in alignment there is a hidden resistance in our energetic fields. Awareness is the key to transforming this misaligned energy. When we are aware of our blockages, we can see what lies beyond the illusion. We can then shift our perspective and see the root of the problem. When we are experiencing misalignment of energy, the most common denominator is that we're being too hard on ourselves.

As human beings, we get accustomed to our unconscious negative beliefs, conditioning, and patterns of behaviour that make us feel small. We tend to live within the box inside our head, but we are more than our physical and mental thoughts. We are expansive and multi-dimensional beings of light and love. We forget who we truly are when we become attached to our illusions.

Steps in Shifting our Blockages:

1. Become aware of the blockage (ie. fear of intimacy, scarcity mentality, victim consciousness, etc.). Ask: What is the mirror?

2. Ask the Universe, God, or your Higher Self: Where is this coming from? What is the root of this blockage?

3. Meditate, reflect, and embrace the cause of the problem. Ask: What is the lesson?

4. Forgive yourself or others. Let go, and release. Ask: Am I ready to let go?

5. Believe that you are being supported by a nurturing Universe. Trust, and have faith in the Divine energy.

6. Self-love is the answer to fear. When we love ourselves, we can then develop the courage to move forward.

7. Be grateful for your blessings and share your gifts with others.

Creating Our Heart's Desires

As I have discovered in my own soul journey, there are many downfalls because we are blinded by our own ego. The separation paradigm that is deeply embedded within our cellular tissues, membranes, memories, and consciousness, needs to heal, so that all the toxicity we have attached to our DNA and spirit can be released. Helping others to remember how to create their heart's desires and reach a level of bliss and inner peace is one of my true passions.

These are the steps in attaining our heart's desires:

1. Sometimes we get confused with what we want to manifest because of other's expectations. Their high expectations about us make us feel like a failure when we don't fit the image that they want to see. We must stop living our life for others, and instead, live our life with passion, doing what we enjoy and love.

2. It is important to know what we want to manifest and create. The Universe will answer when we know and ask for what we want. Visualize that what we desire is already here. This is the power of faith and believing in what we don't see with our physical eyes. As we become aware of our vibrations, we align ourselves with positivity and the highest potential for our dreams to come true. Create a mantra that will help you remember what your soul's purpose is "I allow and accept my Universal soul's purpose to shine, expand, and manifest in my energetic fields. Be it done with love and grace".

3. Awareness is the best tool to know that we are in alignment with our heart's desires. When our heart is open to giving and receiving, the flow of abundance will manifest right into our reality without a doubt. This is the way it is. We are in a dance of synchronized and harmonious events, which are taking place through our magnetism and electromagnetic fields and are resonating at high frequencies of love and light. It's important to be aware of our emotional state so that we can easily shift negativity to positivity before we let it take over our true self and obstruct our truth. Fear is just a shadow that needs light. When love is expressed at its purest form of light, fear dissipates and love is all there is.

4. Action is crucial for our manifestations and creation of our heart's desires. The Universe is in a state of suspended animation and intention collapses the Universal suspension and creates action through the Law of Attraction. Without action there would be no result because attention is where the energy flows and thus brings the form of our thoughts and visions into fruition.

5. Facing challenges as windows of opportunities will help us move forward into another level of understanding. These challenges show us where we are, what we have to do, and where to put our attention to achieve a resolution in our ventures. If we resist that which blocks us, then we can't move forward. So, the secret is to embrace what is blocking us and consciously release the old pattern of our unconscious negative belief, with love and grace.

We are co-creators of our destiny, and our blueprints are encoded in our DNA and existence. As long as the music is still singing in our soul, we will dance in joyful rhythm in this eternal dance with God, the lover of our soul.

CHAPTER 4 | ACTION

Healing Through the Akashic Records

Healing through the Akashic Records is an amazing soul journey. Through working with the Akashic Records we become empowered to rewrite what is written, allowing deep healing to take place. It is a tool for manifesting our highest potential in this lifetime. With the help of the Ascended Masters, Archangels, Angels, and other spiritual guides, we can request access to our soul's Records through the Lords of the Akashic Records. It is in this space, that we can better see and release unconscious negative thoughts, beliefs, and patterns, allowing us to move further into alignment with our soul's purpose. Fear and the lower negative vibrations will be released and awareness will arise, which is the first step in our evolution of consciousness.

There is a sacred prayer which is the pathway through the heart of the Akashic Records. Anyone can attain access when we are vibrationally ready to allow this in our field of space. The people that come in contact with the Akashic Records are souls that are ready to heal in their core being with truth and integrity. The truth is not an easy path but, surely this path will take us to the deepest abyss of our cellular memories, consciousness, and healing of our blood lineages. Healing takes place and we are brought closer to remembrance of who we truly are at the core of our existence. The guides will continue to work with us as long as we journey with them and open our Records. Healing is a process and the more we gain access, the faster we will receive the grace of love and light. Our shadows will be revealed to us and situations will come along as we learn the wisdom and lessons of this lifetime. To be able to release these karmic obstructions in our energetic fields, we have to be able to let go and replace them with new patterns of thoughts, beliefs, and behaviour. As long as we continue to choose the dark side the same situations will repeat themselves in our life's dramas, only with different players. And, if we ignore the inner calling to make positive changes, our life will spiral downward. But it's our freewill to choose if we want to continue to create the cycle of karma and suffering. Why choose that way when we can have access to peace, truth, and love? Energetically, the Ascended Masters and other spiritual guides work at a cellular level. The one who receives the healing will feel this energetic attunements in the present moment. When we consciously and intentionally work on our present situation in this way, we are going to be presented with what we need at this time in our life to move forward with love and grace. The vibrational frequency that we are receiving when we heal in this way is of love and light, it heals the deepest wounds of our soul, layer by layer. Sometimes a vision of a past life may arise that can trigger deep healing in the present moment.

The result of doing this inner healing work evolves you into a conscious being of light: aware, expansive, and enlightened. Miracles manifest right before your eyes, filling your soul with love, joy, and peace. A fulfilled life is when we can see through the drama and suffering and still remain present and balanced within. When we directly experience the essence of our soul, we will suddenly see beyond the veil and find the inner peace that is our birthright. There is no more separation, but oneness with all that is. This arises from the field of unified consciousness.

Alignment of Chakra Energy Centers

When we are tapping into our highest potential, a part of us is triggered to remember that there is more to life than our everyday moments. We begin to remember that we have the power to create the kind of life that we want to have, yet we remain in our comfort zone. Why is that? What does it take to fly and let our dreams come true? We have to unravel the blockages or stumbling blocks in our energetic fields that hinder us from having the life that we desire.

Blockages to release in our Chakra Energy Systems and clues on how they manifest:

1. Root Chakra - this chakra deals with DNA, family and tribal issues, security, stability, foundations, and birthright. When this foundation is not rooted in love and trust, especially with our immediate family, we deal with insecurity. A sense of belonging is lost and we don't feel that we are capable of being loved. The physical symptoms or disease that will manifest in the body will be around the spinal column, teeth, kidneys, legs and immune system.

To release this blockage, we need to have awareness of the function of our Root Chakra and be able to connect to the "issue" or lack of self-love. When we know where the roots of our issues are based, then we can proceed to meditate and ask the Ascended Masters for healing.

Meditation will bring our soul in connection with God, whoever God is for you. The healing energy that is generated will transcend our understanding of why things happen to us in the bigger picture. Go into the Akashic Records and ask for healing in this area, then help others by sharing our gifts of wisdom. The more we share our light, the more light we receive.

2. Sacral Chakra - this chakra is about creativity, power, finances, and relationships. The relationships that we have with our parents will be our compass on how we create a relationship with our lifetime partner. Look back on the dynamic energies of our parents and we may gain insights into the emotional, mental, and spiritual aspects of our life that we need to release and heal in the present moment.

This chakra deals with the Reproductive System and Sexuality. When there is sexual abuse, healing needs to take place at a very deep level, as sexuality and spirituality are in the same energetic level of unification of the soul and spirit in human beings. When this is not respected and the boundary is trespassed, victims will have difficulty seeing themselves as wholesome. Blame, guilt, and self-hatred are common feelings present within the victim. These low vibrations will attract more situations that will bring more abuse because the spirit is like a void that wants to feel love and yet the physical abuse that the person experienced becomes the very weapon of anger towards another human being. There are many hidden, shadows within the victim consciousness.

Ask the Ascended Masters to heal the emotions of anger, revenge, self-destruction, blame, guilt, and self-hatred to be released, cleared, and filled with self-love, kindness, compassion, and forgiveness for oneself and others who have hurt you.

3. Solar Plexus Chakra - this chakra deals with self-trust, gut feelings, intuition, and wisdom. Our intuition lies within the gut feelings that we have when we are in tune with ourselves. Trusting our instincts is very important to our existence as it helps to protect us when we're in dangerous situations. When we don't trust ourselves, we disconnect from our power. People with nervousness are not able to trust themselves and are in fear mode. The low vibrations of anxiety, fear, and suffering are manifested in disease patterns because of all hormonal in-balance. Yoga and meditation are good tools to bring inner strength to this area. We can ask the Ascended Masters to assist us in bringing awareness to our weaknesses and strengthen our Solar Plexus area, connecting us to the power of the Central Sun.

4. Heart Chakra – this chakra is about how we love ourselves and others, relationships, and peace. Our heart is the magnifying force of all that is. We don't exist if our heart stops beating. When we are hurt consciously or unconsciously we develop and build wall upon wall that hinders us from loving unconditionally, and being loved. We are so conditioned to believe that if we don't do certain things we will not be loved. We feel that we have to live up to the expectations of others to feel loved. We have become lost to the true meaning of love because,

deep down, we don't know how to love ourselves. This is why many people engage in an endless cycle of trying to please others for love and validation. Problems that arise from this chakra are mostly situated in the chest such as breast cancer for women and heart attacks for men. Women who stay in toxic relationships develop breast cancer, because they don't fully honour and nurture themselves. Men who don't know how to emote, bury themselves inside an emotional crisis and have heart attacks because they are not in harmony with their circulatory system. We can ask the Ascended Masters to heal our unconscious negative beliefs about ourselves, to forgive those that have hurt us consciously or unconsciously and to receive the love that we deserve.

5. Throat Chakra – this chakra relates to our truth, choice, and voice. When we are suppressing our voice and not able to speak our truth, we are not living at our highest potential. Our voice counts because it comes from our heart resonance. The words that we speak vibrate in the calibration of the truth.

People who have disease in this chakra deal with being suppressed as a child and not having been able to speak up. When there is abuse in the family dynamics, the child grows up with the disability to speak for his or her rights and freedom. The truth will set you free. When we speak the truth, we are aligning to our highest potential because we are no longer hiding in the dark. Our voice is a tool for expressing the light, and by doing so will help others shine their light as well. We can ask the Ascended Masters to heal our abuse, traumatic experiences, and give us the inner strength to speak our truth. Ask Archangel Michael to shine his blue light in the throat chakra for healing.

6. Third Eye Chakra – this chakra is the "veil" that when lifted, allows a person to see beyond form and connects to the bigger picture of our life and soul. It serves as a conduit to see beyond the drama. We connect to our intuition when this chakra is open. It gives us great insight and enhances our physic abilities. Everything that is in front of us is the energy of our own creation. Subconsciously, we manifest whatever we have in our current realities. We have attracted this experience into our life to learn, transform, and grow. What is this person reflecting back to us that we find so agitating? Ask the Ascended Masters to heal whatever darkness or lower vibration we have within to break this pattern of attraction.

Open and activate the Third eye chakra with the assistance of St. Germaine and the Violet Flame to assist in seeing through any illusions.

7. Crown Chakra – this chakra is our connection to the Divine and Cosmic intelligence. Located on the top of our head, the energy of the Seventh Chakra influences the major body systems: central nervous system, muscular system and the skin. Our Crown chakra is our portal to ascension and connects to the Universal and cosmic light coming from the Akashic fields. This transcends our human consciousness and it links us to the Divine source of all that is.

This creative force nourishes the body, mind and spirit. It stores our mystical connections, insights, visions, prophetic thoughts and intuition beyond our human consciousness. We need to ground these in order to balance our physical and spiritual bodies.

The challenge for spiritual people is anchoring this Universal energy, as they find it difficult to ground themselves. Grounding is an important factor in manifestation. We have to align the Universal light within us and anchor this to Mother Earth. By releasing and clearing energies that are toxic to our system and having them transmuted to the core of Mother Earth, we become strong spiritual people. Healing has to take place in all aspects of reality, dealing with the physical, emotional, mental and spiritual traumas. We must connect to all of these aspects of ourselves and align with the Universal energy of love and light. Aligning your column of light creates a wholesome being of love and light anchored to Mother Earth and the spirit of Gaia. Ask the Ascended Masters to heal all traumas from all past incarnated lives, DNA and RNA, crystalline fields, holographic matrices, and bio ethereal fields of your existence to align to your soul's purpose and heart's desires.

Creating Good Patterns of Vibrations

When we want to create, we need to be in sync with the energy capable of manifestation. That energy exists in us right now. However, many of us are not utilizing this energy in an effective way. If we are not happy with the life we have created, then it is obvious that our thoughts, words, and actions, are not in alignment with our truth. When we think and act negatively, we are emitting lower vibrational frequencies which, in turn, will attract lower vibrational experiences into our lives. Knowing that we are responsible for what we attract into our lives, we can let go of playing the role of the victim. The good news is that we have the power to shift and transform our reality by tapping into the Akashic Records. Accessing these records will actually raise our vibration, creating the space needed in order to turn our thoughts and actions into positive energies.

As human beings, we are here to realize who and what we truly are. We are energetic beings of love and light. Some call it soul or spirit that is embodied in the human shell. As a part of awakening to our authentic Self, we need to learn to detach from material belongings. The separation from ourselves and the things we believe we own, forces us back to our spiritual awakening; a shift from external to internal focus. Once that occurs, we begin the integration into understanding Oneness.

This is where deep inner peace lays, when we discover that others are part of our own conscious creation. At this point, we harmonize our thoughts, words, and actions. We start remembering our true calling and connect to the Source of all creation. Our highest potential is to bring light into this world. Light is joy, bliss, love, gratitude, abundance, harmony, and peace. These emotions, along with high vibrations, will create situations that will mirror positive experiences to us. Our perception will shift in the present moment, where creation takes place. Allowing the flow of this positive energy, without resistance, will create miracles right before our eyes.

But how can we help ourselves when we are stuck with negative emotions? First, we need to check in with how we are feeling, right now, in the present moment. We need to look within to identify the triggers that make us react emotionally to others. By doing this, we let go of blame and finding fault with others. We have magnetized everything that is on our plate, so the solution also resides within us. The problems lie deeper in the subconscious and superconscious fields of our energy or consciousness. They lie within our cellular level, DNA and ancestral bloodlines, unconscious negative belief patterns, and conditioning from our family and society. After recognition of these factors, we can start to let go, release, clear, cut the cords of attachment, and seal ourselves with the grids of love and light.

Through identifying and releasing the unconscious patterns within us, we will then tap into our subconscious which holds the vibrations of the collective consciousness of human beings. These are the archetypal energies that are manifesting in our fields. These energies assist us to transcend and tap into the light. The Superconscious is where we want to be when we manifest. This is where the Source of creation lays, the Akashic, or unified field. Everything that is here was first created in this field of light. These vibrations bring this light into our awareness and then manifest into form or experiences.

The two main emotions that human beings experience are fear and/or love. Fear is an illusion, a shadow of energy that needs light. Love is a connection to the Source of creation. It is about being aware and wholesome with unlimited potential and possibilities to create and play in this Universal field. When we feel separation from the Source of love and light, we experience fear. The root of this emotion is the ego's fear of annihilation. It is not easy to wrap our heads around this perception because of our blockages. We mistakenly put attention on negative situations and lose our focus of love. Energy flows where our attention goes, and the more we let go of fear, the more room there is for love to grow.

When we are not feeling good, we are not in our zone. Our natural state is one of being happy and feeling good. This is the time to reflect and check in on which vibrations we are holding. We are all energetic beings, and it is very important to protect our energy fields from energy "vampires", or people who drain us. Often they are unconscious of what they are doing. Regardless, we have to be aware of our energy level so we don't run on empty. We can practice envisioning a light around ourselves or even calling our spiritual guides or angels to protect us wherever we go.

Empaths or people who are very sensitive to energy have gifts of feeling others' pain. It is important that Empaths are aware of their gifts and that they have ways of protecting their energy fields. Empaths can do this by calling on Ascended Master St. Germaine and the Violet flame, along with Archangel Zadkiel for protection.

When we live our lives and experiences vibrating at the high frequencies of love and light that is what we will attract. Believe in the miracles that are going to unfold in this lifetime. When we operate from this vibrational level we can share our gifts of love and light to others and to the world. The Universe will give back whatever is given. As you give, thus you shall receive.

Harmony, Synchronicity, and Miracles

The beautiful fruits of manifestations are the harmonious synchronicities that happen when you are in the zone. What are the signs that you are living in the Universal energy?

- Doors of opportunity open for you

- You become a magnet for attracting events that will lead to your expansion

- You see things in a more magnified way

- Life flows with ease and grace

- You listen to the messages and know that everything is according to Divine timing

- You are living in synchronicity with harmonious creation

- Your relationships become more peaceful, loving, and joyful

- There is a flow of abundance in your life

- You attract miracles

Harmony is the flow of Universal energy. When there is resistance, we create a hindrance in the flow of grace. Open to life and be a channel for this divine grace to flow. We are born to shine our magnificent Self. We are connected to the divine link of God's particles. All of our cellular tissues, fibers, memories, and consciousness are connected to this Source. When we reach this heightened awareness we become one with the Universal mind of

God. We will see others as part of ourselves and ourselves as part of others. We are mirrors of each other.

Synchronicity is a tangible sign that is given by the Universe when we are one with the Source. The Law of One directs us into oneness with all that is. We magnetize others that are resonating in the same vibratory frequency as ourselves. Our high vibration creates a rippling effect in the ocean of love and connects others to our presence. There is communication in the Universal field of energy, and therefore, what we put out there will be received in this unified energetic field of resonance. Everything is energy, and light attracts light. When we are working with the light force, we attract this into our energy field.

Miracles are the fruits of our choices to align ourselves with God or Source. When we are in alignment with Universal energy and the Universal mind of God, we attract miracles into our lives. These are gifts for those who are ready and willing to receive. We have to be open, trusting, and faithful that we have this divine birthright in order for miracles to come. When we believe that miracles do come true, it creates a quantum leap. Everything is here. We are eternal. Believe that what we ask for is already given, then our dreams will come true. Our hopes and desires will be fulfilled in our existence. Dream big and fly high with the angels!

The Law of Integration

In my practice as an Akashic Records healer, I've observed that certain individuals activate downloads of information to me which expand my awareness and understanding. I have a medical doctor who comes to me for consultations from whom I receive download of information. In my sessions with him, and other people, it's like pieces of the puzzle of life come together; this is a metaphorical way of understanding the Law of Integration. I feel that this is the best way to describe this phenomenon, so human beings can understand and apply it with the purpose of reaching their highest path and potential; in order to live fully integrated, wholesome lives, and with clarity of their soul's purpose and existence.

One question that came up from a session was, *"What is the mathematical pattern of existence?"*. When I heard this, there was a big question mark on top of my head. My conscience tells me that this being is asking a big question and how can I possibly address it? Whenever I open the Akashic Records, I totally surrender to whatever answers I receive from my spiritual guides and whatever physical signs I get energetically link the answers to the client's questions. The gift that I have is the visions that I see, whether they are coming from the past, present, or future. I also experience: hearing messages, words of wisdom, feelings of electricity around my energy centers (where it is located is usually where the client needs attention), seeing beings around the person, attachments, interferences or blockages because of unresolved issues of forgiveness from another being. I experience signs and symbols, colours around the auric fields, and/or sparkling crystalline forms around the auric fields. These are examples of my experiences and what I receive when I open the Akashic Records of human beings. Additionally, in the days leading up to a healing with a client I will receive downloads of information and wisdom on how I can assist or help transcend this person. In regards to the question on the mathematical pattern of existence, the Doctor created the theory according to the visions that I received and simplified it "Whatever you do in the Universal connection approaching perfection, you are tuning in to the mathematical patterns of existence. It is your only path to actually access these patterns, there is no other way. The instrument of perfection is irrelevant. it is the attempt to achieve perfection by whatever means which is what is important. The process of balancing the forces is in fact the mathematical pattern. It's not what you see or think it is, but rather the interpretation. If you are not living your life with integrity, the other parts of your life can not be interpreted. Integrity is the source of all connection to the Divine source or infinite intelligence. It's not the individual life that matters, it's the pattern of how they are put together that explains why they are important and how they function."

I ask the Doctor for a further simpler explanation and I received this answer; "Whatever work you do in this lifetime, may it be a nurse or a garbage collector, doesn't matter, but what does matters is the attempt to do your best with integrity that connects you to the Divine source and Universal connection". Thus, it is the Law of Integration that holds our harmonious creation in every relationship that we encounter in our lives. Our lives were designed to be simple, but we make them complicated. This is what happens when we live inside our head: we hear many voices. These voices become our escape from facing reality. They lead us away from what truly is important in our simple lives. Thus, the situation exists that we are living inside this box that defines our limitations and constricts our understanding of what is. Somehow or another we have forgotten the way out of this trap created by our own ego and illusions. Our heart and conscience, which is where our soul resides, is the aspect of our integrity which connects us to this vast Universe of creations.

Furthermore, I met another healer who had consultations with me and while he was in front of me I had visions of 12 strands of connections like the 12 strands of DNA of our multi-dimensional selves. These explained the blueprint for manifestation in accordance with the Universal Laws. I realized that these formations or functions connect according to the theory of the Law of Integration. They are as follows:

1. Divinity or Oneness

2. Creation or Genesis

3. Womb of Creation or Darkness

4. Light

5. Sound or Vibration

6. Sacred Geometry

7. Archetypal Blueprints

8. Ego or Separation/ Polarity or Duality

9. Energy

10. Thoughts

11. Words

12. Deeds or Action

I call these the Blueprints for Manifestation in accordance to the Universal Laws. We integrate these functions into our realities to be wholesome, harmonious, empowered, and evolved light beings. These are the formations and functions that are necessary in our Human consciousness. When we reach this bliss or mystical unification with the Absolute and Cosmic Universe, we will experience boundless, timeless, cosmic, and Universal connection to the patterns of existence as the infinitesimal souls that we are. There is no time and space in the field of oneness; it is as it is--the present moment. We are co-creators of this expansive universe of ourselves, upholding the truth with the intention of integrating with 'all that is' in our unified consciousness of our Universal souls. We are part of the Universal laws that govern our existence and when we see clearly, or become conscious of these laws, we become fully conscious light beings who anchor the Universal and cosmic light into the heart of Mother Earth/Gaia.

As I gather and receive more information, a Master of Engineering and Physics told me that these functions or formations that I'm referring to in regards to the Law of Integration are actually based on what they call the Sum Rule of Integration. These functions or formations are actually the parts of all the dimensions of x, y, z, or summation. And all of them make up this integration; therefore 'S' (oneness or divinity) $= Sx + Sy + Sz$ (summation of all formations or functions), which you can confirm in Wikipedia. In Calculus the Sum Rule of Integration states that the integral of the sum of two functions is equal to the sum of their integrals. It is of particular use for the integration of sums and is one part of the linearity of integration. When I look at the bigger picture of this Law of Integration, it actually connects Science and Spirituality by explaining how the Universal Laws affect us in every way. The wisdom arises in understanding how they operate and affect us, making a big difference to our electro-magnetic fields. The force of the Universe affects all that is within and around us. It affects the macro and micro of all sentient beings and how we operate in one holographic field of the Matrix. The sum of 'all that is', is actually within us and our cellular consciousness when we still our minds and enter into the flow of the river of consciousness. There is no separation in this blissful space of unconditional love. There is only what is, and whatever is in our fields is 'all that is'. There is no judgment or attachment to the outcome or expectation of anything, but only what is in the present moment. We are both the creation of the cosmos and co-creators of our realities.

The collective consciousness and Universal archive of infinite possibilities is the Akashic fields of your Records.

Honour and empower yourself as gifts of the stars to Earth from Heaven!

ABOUT THE AUTHOR

In IONS of Manifestation, Teza Zialcita shares simple yet profound steps for manifesting all of our hearts' desires and more. She approaches the topic masterfully, both simplifying the process, yet at the same time fully honouring the profound holistic nature of this work. Manifestation is an art form that requires our whole heart, soul and life to be engaged with a higher purpose and a sense of interconnectedness to all that is. Through Teza's graceful teachings, this great opportunity is accessible to all. After reading this book, there is no turning back!

Teza's process is clear and effective; The Intention, Vision, Attention, and Action formula aligns our soul with the Universal blueprint of creation, so that we can gracefully dance in the flow of manifestation. This way, we will constantly amaze ourselves as our creation expands to wondrous new levels. Through this process, we learn to evolve beyond the personal, into a Universal way of life. We can lovingly and consciously clear blockages and work with our emotions, for the highest good of ourselves and all sentient beings.

We are unlimited creators, free to create a life of true freedom, bliss and awakening.

The time is now...and truly, we are the "ONE" we've been waiting for!

Other books by the Author

<u>Universal Conscious Self: Simple Steps to Connect to Your True Essence</u>

Universal Conscious Self reestablishes your connection to your Source and Divine Self. The intention is to help you move beyond your egoic mind and pay attention to your own divinity by living through your heart and reconnecting to your divine essence. You are a multi-dimensional being of light and love in an expansive and infinitesimal Universe.

Techniques are given to experience more joy, peace, and love, including breaking free from karmic bonds and heal from inner childhood trauma; healing and letting go of anger and fear; transcending negativity and victim consciousness; and remembering your oneness to others and Source.

Teza discusses the importance of cultivating your relationship to Source and your oneness to others through inner awareness and unconditional love. By doing so, you are able to achieve a different way of being and thus live through your expansive self through the heart and allow for Universal guidance to flow and enrich your life. You are able to achieve happiness and peace within that is deeply rooted to Source, while remembering the importance of the role you have chosen to play in this universe and how you can impact it by focusing on your inner beauty and self.

Find out more about Teza at:

http://akashic-soul-healing.com/

https://www.facebook.com/tezamysticangel

Email address: teza.akashicsoulhealing@gmail.com

Made in the USA
Columbia, SC
13 October 2017